HOLIDAY ENCORES

By Glenda Austin

ISBN 978-1-4950-6611-5

WILLIS MUSIC

EXCLUSIVELY DISTRIBUTED BY

HAL•LEONARD®
CORPORATION
7777 W. BLUEMOUND RD. P.O. BOX 13819 MILWAUKEE, WI 53213

Visit Hal Leonard Online at
www.halleonard.com

PREFACE

Holiday Encores came about quite by accident. As a music teacher, I arrive early practically every day. One morning, having all my plans prepared and ready, I had some extra time. Not knowing exactly what possessed me, I made a little video on my iPhone of a song my elementary students were singing. It was "Over the River and Through the Wood." I played it pretty much the way I do when they sing it, improvising as I went along. Then I decided to post the video on my Facebook page. Surprisingly, I received a lot of likes and comments, and they were favorable!

That was the beginning of me posting little "snippets" on Facebook. Every piece in this collection has been recorded and posted. Many people asked if the arrangements were in print and available for purchase, so I am thrilled to share with you this short collection of some of my favorite seasonal music. Even though I have notated them to the best of my ability, beware that there could be a note or two in the recordings that you don't see in print. Or, vice-versa! That's the nature of improvising: to compose or play on the spur of the moment. Because they are joyful, unique, and short, the arrangements make for perfect encores on recital programs or at a holiday gathering with friends and family. I played through them all just today and each one made me smile, remembering the fun I had recording them.

If you are on Facebook, check them out on my page. They are still there. And one more thing: be sure to notice my makeshift theatrical props. I had almost as much fun figuring out what to use as I did writing the arrangements!

Glenda Austin

P.S. Be looking for more snippets—you never know when the next one will appear!

BIO

Glenda Austin is a composer, arranger, pianist, and teacher. She has taught music classes in public and private schools for over 30 years and performs regularly in local theater, church, and school settings. An active clinician for Willis Music, Glenda has presented her music regionally, nationally, as well as in Canada and Japan. She and her husband David live in Joplin, Missouri.

CONTENTS

Over the River and Through the Wood

Traditional
Arranged by Glenda Austin

Up on the Housetop

Words and Music by B.R. Hanby
Arranged by Glenda Austin

I Saw Three Ships

Traditional English Carol
Arranged by Glenda Austin

Jolly Old St. Nicholas

Traditional 19th Century American Carol
Arranged by Glenda Austin

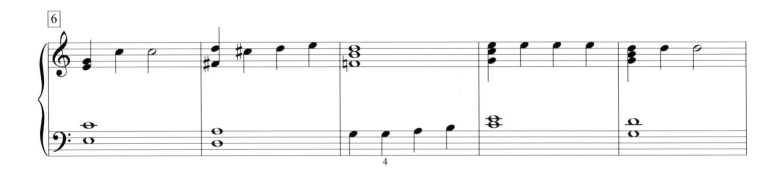

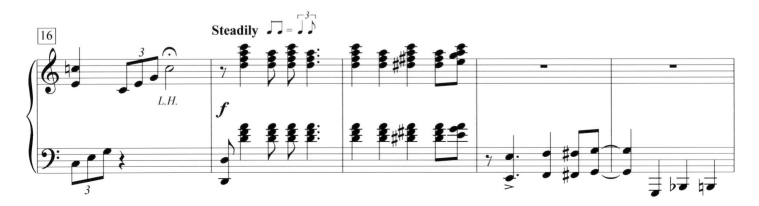

We Gather Together

Words from *Nederlandtsch Gedenckclanck*
Netherlands Folk Melody
Arranged by Edward Kremser
Adapted by Glenda Austin

In a classical style

With very light pedal

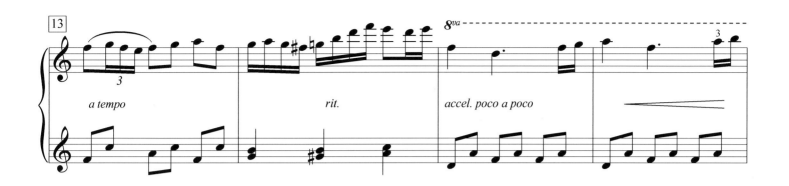

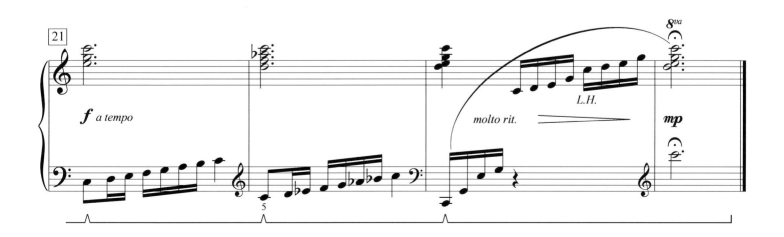

We Three Kings of Orient Are

Words and Music by John H. Hopkins, Jr.
Arranged by Glenda Austin

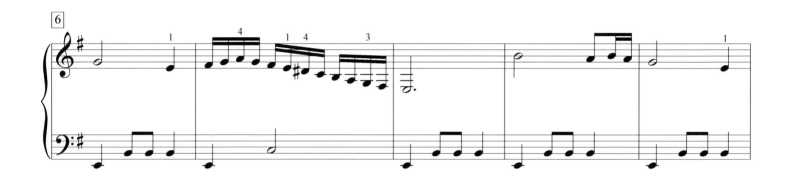

Jingle Bells

Words and Music by J. Pierpont
Arranged by Glenda Austin

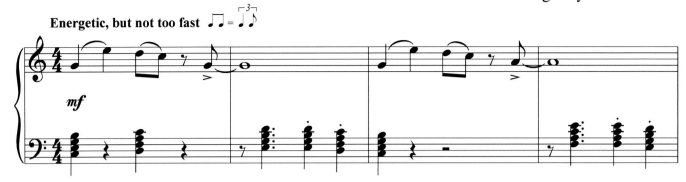

Silent Night

Words by Joseph Mohr
Music by Franz X. Gruber
Arranged by Glenda Austin